MINI-GUIDES

MW00609528

ARMOR IN NORMANDY: THE AMERICANS...

June - August 1944

by Alexandre THERS

Lay-out by the author - Computer drawings by Antoine POGGIOLI
Translated from the French by Jonathan NORTH

PARIS

AMERICAN ARMOR IN 1944

Unlike the British, the Americans were constantly expanding their armored units throughout 1943 and 1944. Indeed, by the end of the war there would be 16 armored divisions. By 1944 American economic muscle ensured they would play the leading role in the allied coalition. It would be their standard tank, the Sherman, which would form the backbone not only of the Americans' own divisions but also those fielded by their allies.

AMERICAN ARMORED DIVISIONS IN 1944

Experience gained from the battlefields of 1943 made it quite clear to the Americans that they would have to undertake a thorough reorganization of their armored units. It seemed the divisions were top heavy with tanks and that infantry and artillery were lacking. The British divisions had evolved their theory so that they could give maximum priority to exploitation. The Americans thought long and hard about the tank's role and eventually based their theory on the fact that a tank - in this case the Sherman - could act as both an infantry support vehicle and an assault vehicle since it combined armor, firepower and speed.

In 1943 the US divisions were therefore reformed in a radical reorganization. There would now be two types of division. The first was the heavy armored division (with 14,620 men and 390 tanks), composed of a three-battalion regiment of medium tanks and a two-battalion regiment of light tanks. The second was the light armored division (10,937 men and 263 tanks) composed of three battalions of tanks, three of infantry and three artillery groups. The divisions were brigaded into Combat Commands (A and B), which were designed to add flexibility and increase mobility. There were also the Reserve Command, the Artillery Command and the Transport Command. The two Combat Commands were the ones which could deliver the punch. They themselves were divided into constituent elements (companies and battalions). A tank battalion consisted of three companies of medium tanks, a company of light tanks, and a support company. Mechanized infantry, formed into three battalions, would act in support. In addition, there was the artillery. Each battalion of field artillery comprised eighteen 105 mm M7 self-propelled guns.

There might also be tank destroyers and battalions of anti-aircraft guns could also be permanently attached to the armored units. Individual battalions of tanks might also serve detached from the divisions, acting perhaps to reinforce larger formations.

The theory was that the Sherman would not actually be pitched into battle against enemy armor but that this task would be left to the tank destroyers (the realities of the battlefield soon made it clear that this was an erroneous point of view). The tanks themselves would be reserved for the rapid exploitation of any breakthrough. This armored doctrine was in contrast to the view held by the Germans, who used their armor on a grand scale. German tanks, forming a solid, mobile mass, were grouped in order to overcome any resistance - whether armored or not - and then to quickly exploit any resulting breakthrough. So it was that, again in contrast to the Germans, the Americans refrained from deploying armored corps or tank armies.

EQUIPMENT

As we have seen, the principal tank employed by the Americans was the Sherman. It was a medium tank and the US Army always proved reluctant to develop a heavier substitute. The Sherman's development was pretty much complete by 1944. But the Americans deployed a greater variety of other vehicles in other categories. There were light tanks, tank destroyers, armored cars and a vast multitude of specialist vehicles within tank battalions, tank-destroying battalions, reconnaissance squadrons attached to cavalry units or units attached to infantry divisions. In addition, there were the ubiquitous Half-Tracks, light vehicles serving throughout the Army in a variety of roles. Armor utilized in Normandy could fall into the following categories:

Assault Tanks

Essentially, variants of the Sherman equipped with 75 mm or 76.2 mm gun in a revolving turret. Designed to be as versatile as possible, the tanks could perform as support for infantry as well as assault vehicles for use against non-armored units.

Reconnaissance Tanks

These light tanks were deployed against a variety of obstacles such as machine gun nests or anti-tank positions. Fast and flexible, such vehicles were also cheaper and easier to produce and they therefore took on greater importance. Initially used in an offensive capacity, they were later employed more and more on the defensive as the war progressed.

Tank Destroyers

These were never highly regarded by the US Army, something probably attributable to the uncertainty of how they should be employed. In appearance they were similar to tanks and this probably accounts for their being used as such, even though they proved vulnerable to enemy fire. Even though they were not always satisfactory, aside, perhaps, from the M18 Hellcat, they played a vital role throughout the Normandy campaign. While their guns ensured that they fulfilled their role as anti-tank weapons, their inferior armor and their open-topped turrets rendered them very vulnerable to infantry and mortar attacks. Although not as heavy as most assault tanks, they were faster. They proved adept at ambushes and working in a support capacity but they were less useful during the offensives mounted in the summer of 1944.

Overall American armor suffered from a number of drawbacks. The Sherman proved a worthy opponent to the Panzer IV, its German counterpart and rival. It could also take on the Sturmgeschütz III, an assault gun. But when it came to heavier armor, the Sherman was simply outclassed by the Tiger and the Panther except in terms of reliability and mobility. When it comes to looking at tank destroyers, then the M10 did good service, without being exceptional, and sometimes outclassed the Panzer IV. The Hellcat, on the other hand, had nothing to fear from any enemy armor and it earned a tremendous reputation among the Germans. Unfortunately it was not available in large numbers during the Normandy campaign and even then it arrived pretty late on the scene.

The American advantage lay, like that of their British allies, in the numbers they could employ, in the supply of fuel they could rely on, in the rapid replacement of destroyed material, and in the omnipresent power of Allied aircraft.

THE CONTEXT

The American sectors established in Normandy were particularly unsuited for the conduct of armored warfare. The Americans disembarked along the bottom of the Cotentin peninsula and found that as they tried to exit from Omaha they either found themselves in marshy terrain or frustrated by cliffs. Worse was to follow inland. There the terrain became even more difficult and the Americans discovered that the chief characteristic of this part of Normandy was the so-called 'bocage' country. This consisted of a series of fields, each surrounded by thick hedgerows and separated by twisted, sunken roads or tracks. This made the terrain unsuitable for tanks and made setting an ambush easy. Furthermore, when tanks attempted to break through the hedgerows they exposed their underbellies, that part of a tank most vulnerable to enemy fire.

Patton's tactics combined a mixed force of infantry and armor, all mobile, supported by artillery, engineers and signal troops. Patton, acting in concert with Allied aircraft, therefore was personally in charge of a combined force of all arms. This was coordinated, as much as possible by means of radio communication. Each commander could keep in touch with his counterparts, communicate his orders and retain control of the battle. This was vital, especially when fighting in a fluid and open situation, something of a trademark for Patton's Third Army as they enjoyed continual success. But armored divisions were also capable of fighting a defensive battle.

The Americans deployed six armored divisions as well as independent armored battalions designed to operate in conjunction with the infantry. In all perhaps 2,000 Shermans, some of which were equipped with the 76.2 mm and reinforced armor, took to the field. These were further reinforced in August when the French armored divisions arrived and added their weight. These were organized and equipped in the American manner.

THE 'DUPLEX DRIVE' SHERMAN

Perhaps the most unusual Sherman variant was the amphibious Duplex Drive (DD) based on the M4A1 75 or the M4A1 (75) W.

A rear view of a Duplex Drive with its flotation skirt deployed. Making the idea reality was down to the engineer Nicholas Straussler.

....

B elow: Inflating the flotation skirt on a Duplex Drive took around 15 minutes. Here, the hem of the skirt has been lifted to reveal the rubber tubes, which gave the screen its rigidity. (IWM)

....

R ight: A sleeve badge belonging to a member of the US Navy's amphibious forces. It represents an alligator pouring forth tanks. (Militaria Magazine)

The tank was fitted with a flotation skirt constructed out of 30 rubber tubes. These allowed the tank to actually float. It could be launched from a boat and could traverse a relatively short distance to the coast. Twin propellers connected to the tank's motor guaranteed the tank a speed of 6 km/h over a calm sea. The propellers could be operated whilst the skirt was inflated by means of a lever, which was connected to the propellers by a series of rods. The actual term Duplex Drive stems from the mechanical transmission, which enabled the engine to be switched from powering the twin propellers to powering the sprocket wheels. The tank's flotation skirt meant that it could float to the shore, once there, the skirt was deflated and its engine reverted to acting normally. One of the advantages of the DD was that the front of the inflatable skirt could be lowered to allow the tank to make use of its gun, even while it was in the water.

Its interior was replete with all the usual equipment - engine, transmission, weapons, ammunition and equipment - but also contained hydraulic pumps, and the controls which operated the skirt and the propellers.

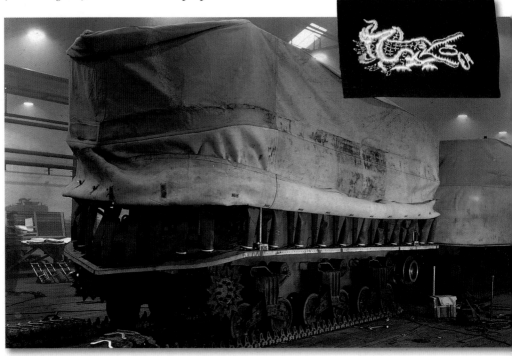

TECHNICAL DATA

Crew: 5
Combat weight: 30.3 tons
Engine: Continental R975 C1, 9-cylinder gasoline engine, 400 hp
Max. speed on road: 34 km/h
Range on road: 193 km
Fuel capacity: 796 liters
Armament: 1 x 75 mm M3 gun, 2 x 7.62 mm M1919 A4 machineguns, 1 x 12.7 mm M2HB anti-aircraft MG
Ammunition: 97 shells, 5050 MG rounds
Armor thickness (max. without mantlet): 51 mm at 56°
Radio: SCR 508/528/538

*R*ight: The M13 periscope or episcope used by the Sherman. (Overlord Collection)

*O*pposite: The great advantage of the DD system was that it didn't burden the tank unnecessarily. (IWM)

A Duplex Drive Sherman with its skirt deflated. The skirt would be kept rigid by the 36 inflatable tubes but also by foldable metal rods. *(Illustration by Jean Restayn)*

Among all the special equipment should be mentioned the electronic pumps which jettisoned water from the tank by means of compressed air. All this extra machinery seriously reduced the amount of space within the tank.

The DD was classified at the time as a secret weapon. Crews were formed and trained in March 1944. One of the first things with which they were made familiar, was the tank's respiratory equipment which was so vast that it considerably reduced the chance of any man escaping from its hatches.

THE 'SHERMAN'

This American medium tank was the mainstay of the US and British armored forces and it was probably manufactured more than any other. There were five basic versions including the M4, M4A1 and, later, the M4A3. All these were employed in Normandy.

It was a simple design, robust, reliable, fast and easy to maintain. All this made it extremely popular among tank crews and mechanics. It had other advantages too, including the excellent Wright Continental engine (although the M4A3 was provided with a Ford V8), and had an automatic gearbox and transmission.

The ammunition (on the wet version) was protected in cases lined with glycerin and water which reduced the risk of fire should the tank be hit and it had an excellent intercom system for communication.

The turret could rotate 360 degrees and housed a gun, which is gyro-stabilized in elevation. This ability to rotate made it superior to similar German tanks, but the tank's rate of fire was also faster (20 rounds a minute). The Sherman could be fitted with a variety of tracks to enable it to cross different types of terrain. Its chief weapon was the 75 mm gun with a maximum range of 3,000m although this was reduced by half when firing penetration rounds.

These rounds did not achieve sufficient velocity at close range making it extremely difficult for the Shermans to be effective at close range against German heavy tanks. The M4A176 (W), a version equipped with the 76.2 mm, also saw the light of day. Although outgunned by the Panther, the M4

A M4A2 Sherman belonging to General Leclerc's 2nd Armored Division. This model of Sherman was instantly recognizable thanks to the driver's hatch and that of the co-driver. The 75 mm gun had a M34A1 mantle with a built-in machine gun. (©ECPAD/France)

....

R ight: A leather protective helmet as worn by American tank crews. (Private collection)

....

B elow: The Sherman was distinguished by its single-cast hull but it could have additional armor bolted on to the glacis plate and along the tank's sides. (National Archives)

TECHNICAL DATA

Crew: 5
Combat weight: 30.3 tons
Engine: Continental R975 C1,
9-cylinder gasoline engine,
400 hp
Max. speed on road: 39 km/h
Range on road: 193 km
Fuel capacity: 796 liters
Length: 5.8 m
Width: 2.6 m
Height: 2.74 m
Armament: 1 x 75 mm M3
gun, 2 x 7.62 mm M1919
A4 machineguns,
1 x 12.7 mm M2HB anti-
aircraft machinegun
Ammunition: 97 shells,
5050 MG rounds
Armor thickness
(max. without mantlet):
51 mm at 56°
Radio: SCR 508/528/538

*Opposite: A Sherman with
an M1 76.mm gun. Tanks thus
equipped began to replace those
with 75mms in July 1944.
Even so, its anti-tank capability
was only marginally better
than the M3 75 mm.
(RR)*

*An M4 Sherman. The majority of the tanks to land in Normandy were M4s
or M4A1s. Both of these variants were armed with the 75 mm M3.
The chief difference between the M4 and M4A1 was in their hull.
In the former it was welded together but the latter's was cast
as a single piece.
(Illustration by Jean Restayn)*

....

*Right: A Sherman's track plate.
(J. P. André Collection)*

compensated with its numerical superiority and its
reliability.

Unfortunately the tank also suffered from poor
armor and the alarming propensity to 'brew-up'
when hit.

THE M4 AND M4A3 'SHERMAN' (105 mm)

This tank was designed to provide heavy artillery support and, equipped with a 105 mm gun, it came into service with the American Army in 1943.

It made use of an M4 or M4A3 chassis with a 47-degree slope. The turret was modified to house a 105 mm howitzer, an M4 on an M52 gun mount with modified sights. A hatch was placed on top of the turret so the gun-loader could enter and exit. The gun had no gyrostabilizer and the turret had no rotate engine. The elevation of the gun varying between 33 and -10 degrees. The tank carried 68 rounds divided into three types: high explosive, anti-tank (the M67 HEAT), explosive (the M1 HE) and smoke (the M84 Smoke). The anti-tank round could pierce armor 100 mm thick but again, it had poor initial velocity on account of the gun's trajectory, making the tank unsuitable for an anti-tank role. Instead, it came into its own against bunkers. Its rate of fire was only eight rounds a minute.

This American magazine cover plays tribute to US armored troops.
(P. Charbonnier Collection)

Below: An M4 Sherman (105) photographed in August 1944. Its most distinguishing feature was probably the new glacis plate, angled at 47 degrees. The use of glycerin and water to protect the tank's ammunition was, however, now discontinued. (National Archives)

TECHNICAL DATA

(M4A3-105)

Crew: 5
Combat weight: 30.5 tons
Engine: Ford GAA,
8-cylinder gasoline engine,
500 hp
Max. speed on road: 42 km/h
Range on road: 160 km
Fuel capacity: 764 liters
Length with gun: 5.91 m
Width: 2.62 m
Height: 2.74 m
Armament: 1 x 105 mm M4
howitzer, 2 x 7.62 mm M1919
A4 machineguns, 1 x 12.7 mm
M2HB anti-aircraft
machinegun
Ammunition: 68 shells,
5650 MG rounds
Armor thickness (max.
without mantlet): 63 mm at 47°
Radio: SCR 508/528/538

*O*pposite: An M4 being put
through its paces by the
Armored Board at Fort Knox.
Modifications carried out whilst
the tank was actually entering
production were relatively few.

*T*he tank's crew was positioned as follows: the driver was at the fore of the vehicle,
on the left; his assistant, who also operated the machine gun, was on the right;
the tank commander was in the turret, at the back and to the right, with the gunner
just in front of him and the loader on the left. (Illustration by Jean Restayn)

The first tanks came into service in February 1944 and were distributed
among the tank battalions. Each battalion received six. The tanks were regu-
larly employed at the head of advancing columns as they had
been provided with thicker frontal armor than the basic
Shermans. The British received 593 tanks of this type.

*O*pposite: A machine-gun cover used to protect
the forward machine gun on the glacis plate.
(J. P. André Collection)

(Bovington Tank Museum)

11

THE SHERMAN 'TANKDOZER'

The Sherman chassis was an excellent base for all kinds of transformations. It gave rise to a number of Sherman variants equipped with different engines.

A Tankdozer belonging to the 63d Engineer Battalion. (National Archives)

Below: A Tankdozer at Tribehou on July 25, 1944. (National Archives)

Below: Tankdozers were crewed by personnel drawn from the 601st Engineer Light Equipment Company and the 741st and 743rd Tank Battalions. (Militaria Magazine)

There was the M4A1 (76) W with its 76.2 mm gun designed to improve its performance against tanks and then there was the minesweeping Flail tank, the M32 breakdown tank, the Duplex Drive amphibious tank and the bulldozer. One Sherman variant was equipped with a 105 mm gun which could support an assault by throwing a shell 11.5 km, obliterating defensive positions. It came into service in February 1944. But one of the variants played a key role during the American landings in Normandy on June 6, 1944. It was, alongside with the Duplex Drive, the M1 Tankdozer. It was designed by American engineers shortly before the landings took place and was based on the M4. Its chief role on the D-Day was to destroy the obstacles the Germans had constructed on the landing beaches. It boasted a large bulldozer scoop, raised or lowered by hydraulic jacks. The addition of this scoop added 3,600kg to the tank's weight, but, on the other hand, it provided the tank with an additional layer of armor allowing it to push into enemy defenses with relative impunity. The crew was certainly more fortunate than the drivers of the more ordinary bulldozers who also operated on the beachheads. The Tankdozers were employed as part of the Gap Assault Teams and were given the task of cutting a breach through the German defenses. Theoretically, each Assault Team made use of one Tankdozer, each one of which towed a trailer loaded with 250kg

A n electric lamp as used onboard a Tankdozer. (J. P. André Collection)

A Tankdozer belonging to the US 3rd Armored Division takes part in Operation Cobra towards the end of July 1944. (National Archives).

W ith waves of troops hitting the beaches on June 6, the destruction of obstacles was a relatively complex issue. It was down to the Tankdozers to blast a way through. (Illustration by Jean Restayn)

of explosive. But of the 16 tanks which were assigned to Omaha Beach, only six actually gained the shore and one of these was without its bulldozer scoop.

THE M8 HOWITZER MOTOR CARRIAGE

Built on the chassis of the M5 light tank, this little mobile howitzer was designed to support infantry companies (in tank battalions or cavalry reconnaissance squadrons).

The M8's hull was entirely sealed, modifications having been made which closed the escape hatches normally found above the driver's head. He could now reach his post through the open gun turret. In addition, the driver and his assistant now had hatches cut into the armor in front of them for forward vision as well as a periscope and an episcope. The turret of the M8 was open on top and housed a short 75 mm M1, M2 or M3 howitzer with a 360-degree field of fire. The vehicle's armor afforded the crew little protection and the M8 was frequently used as a support vehicle called up by company HQs.

Space within the vehicle was extremely limited so the tank's chassis was modified to allow it to tow the M10 munitions trailer. Just like the Sherman, various tracks could be fitted. The M8 had a good rate of fire, some 25 rounds a minute with a maximum range of around 5 miles. Each squadron was composed

A *ugust 1944, an M8 belonging to the French 2e Division Blindée heads towards the Orne. (Bovington Tank Museum)*

R *ight: An M5 driving sprocket. (J. P. André Collection)*

B *elow: The M8's mantle allowed an elevation of between +40 and -20 degrees, much better than all of its rivals. (National Archives)*

This howitzer belongs to the 33rd Armored Regiment, part of the 3rd Armored Division. (Illustration by Jean Restayn)

TECHNICAL DATA

Crew: 4
Combat weight: 15.5 tons
Engine: 2 x Cadillac series 42, 8-cylinder gasoline engine, 148 hp
Max. speed on road: 58 km/h
Range on road: 161 km
Fuel capacity: 405 liters
Length: 4.84 m
Width: 2.29 m
Height: 2.7 m including MG
Armament: 1 x 75 mm M2 or M3 howitzer, 1 x 12.7 mm M2HB machinegun
Ammunition: 46 shells, 400 MG rounds
Armor thickness (max.): 44 mm
Radio: SCR 510

of 6 vehicles. Actual production had ceased just before the Normandy landings. The M8 gave good service in Normandy but was progressively replaced from mid-1944 by the 105 mm howitzer mounted on the Sherman chassis.

Above right: R14 headphones as used in the M8. (J. P. André Collection)

Opposite: This view from above reveals the true scale of the turret. The turret's size meant that there could be no escape hatches for the driver or co-driver. (Bovington Tank Museum)

THE HMC M7
SELF-PROPELLED GUN

This mobile howitzer was built using an M4 Sherman chassis and was used to give flexible artillery support to infantry units.

A convoy of M7s trundles through Great Britain shortly before D-Day. The Americans had little mobile artillery, the M7 being one of a small number of such weapons available in 1944. The M7 supported the landings, providing covering fire as the troops headed for the shore. (National Archives)

B elow: The Priest's degree of elevation ranged from 35 degrees to -5 degrees. This was less than a field howitzer's but this was because the recoil of the Priest's gun could damage the vehicle if it tilted too far. (National Archives)

The M7 was fitted with a 105 mm howitzer in a particularly unusual way: right down the central axis of the vehicle. To its right was position a machine-gun cupola, raised like a kind of pulpit. This might explain the Priest nickname bestowed on the vehicle by the British. Certain versions had permanent reserve fuel tanks fitted as part of the vehicle's structure. The armor plating to the fore of the vehicle could be raised or lowered. The driver's forward vision was through a hatch cut in the armor plating, as well as a protoscope which could be covered in bad weather with a windshield. The vehicle was open on top and the engine was designed so that the vehicle could keep up with the most mobile armored vehicles.

The M7 was a sound piece of equipment combining firepower with good protective armor. It met with considerable success and was used in great numbers by Allied forces. Some were converted to radio vehicles, guaranteeing communication between vehicles or pinpointing targets for other Priests. The M7 chassis was the basis for a transport variant used by the British and Canadians - the Unfrocked Priest, extrapolated from the Kangaroo.

The Priest carried three types of ammunition: high explosive, anti-tank (the M67 HEAT),

O pposite: This piece of equipment measured the degree of elevation for field artillery, including the M7. (C. Thers Collection)

A typical crew for a Priest consisted of around 12 men. Six of these were regarded as reserves; the others served the vehicle and the gun. Three men were required to aim, load and fire the gun, the driver, his assistant and the gunner would supply ammunition, bringing up shells and preparing it for the gun crew. For example, shot was divided up into groups numbered between one and seven according to projectile weight. If, for example, a four was chosen, it would be brought forwards and placed in a specific point ready for the gunners. The reserve could be called upon should the vehicle's ammunition be seriously depleted.
(Illustration by Jean Restayn)

TECHNICAL DATA

(M7 - M7B1)

Crew: 7
Combat weight: 23 tons
Engine: Continental R975 C1, 9-cylinder gasoline engine, 400 hp or a Ford GAA, 8-cynlinder gasoline engine, 500n hp.
Max. speed on road: 39 km/h
Max speed across country: 24 km/h
Range on road: 200 km
Range across country: 136 km
Fuel capacity: 662 liters
Length: 6 m
Width: 2.87 m
Height: 2.95 m
Armament: 1 x 105 mm M2A1 howitzer, 1 x 12.7 mm M2HB machinegun
Ammunition: 69 shells, 300 MG rounds
Armor thickness (max.): 38 mm

explosive (the M1 HE) and smoke (the M84 Smoke). There were 24 in each heavy armor division's artillery battalion. The same number was assigned to those in light armored divisions and six were in each armored battalion.

*R*ight: Cloth and leather gloves of the type used by gun crews. These allowed the crew to remove the shell casing after firing the gun.
(National Archives)

*R*ight: Between April 1944 and May 1945 some 3,000 Priests were produced. The one pictured here is one of the older variants.
(National Archives)

The M12 Gun Motor Carriage

This imposing self-propelled gun, nicknamed King Kong at the time, was one of the first such vehicles to be developed by the Americans. The concept was to provide the Army with mobile heavy artillery support.

The M12 took as its basis the chassis of the M3 Lee medium tank. Adaptations were made, including the use of Sherman tracks and rollers, but the most significant change was the relocation of the engine from the rear of the vehicle to the front. This gave a better equilibrium. The vehicle carried the excellent M1918 (or M1917) 155 mm gun, a weapon identical to the French 155 GPF. There was a ramp to the rear of the vehicle and this was lowered when the gun went into action to improve stability.

The M12 was not just capable of stopping German armor in its tracks; it could also destroy emplacements and defenses up to 9 km away. In a direct hit, its high explosive shells could penetrate 2 m of concrete from a distance of between 1000 - 2000 m.

An M30 munitions transporter used an M12 chassis. The space made available after the removal of the gun allowed it to carry 40 shells whilst the M12 could only accommodate 10. (Bovington Tank Museum)

Right: A T51 rubber-coated track as used by Shermans and the M5. (J. P. André Collection)

Below: A battery in action in the summer of 1944. The ramp at the back also served as a step. (Bovington Tank Museum)

Some 74 M12s were transported to the Normandy coast in June 1944 but not all were operational on D-Day. (Illustration by Jean Restayn)

TECHNICAL DATA

Crew: 6
Combat weight: 27 tons
Engine: Continental R975 C1, 9-cylinder gasoline engine, 400 hp
Max. speed on road: 39 km/h
Max speed across country: 20 km/h
Range on road: 230 km
Fuel capacity: 757 liters
Length: 6.73 m without gun and folding shovel
Width: 2.67 m
Height: 2.88 m
Armament: 1 x 155 mm M1917 or M1917A or M1918M1 gun
Ammunition: 10 shells
Armor thickness (max.): 51 mm

Above right: The American helmet M1 is also worn by the crews of mechanized artillery. (Militaria Magazine)

....

Opposite: An M12 carried a crew of 12 men. There were six in the M12 itself and a further six manning the attached munitions transporter, the M30. (Bovington Tank Museum)

The M12 was often accompanied by the M30 Cargo Carrier built using the same chassis but with the gun removed, enabling the M30 to transport a vast number of 155 mm shells.

Despite its evident merits, the M12 got the cold shoulder from the American military authorities. They initially assumed they had no need of a weapon of this type but then realized how useful the vehicle would be in Normandy. In 1943 six battalions of heavy artillery were eventually fitted out with the M12 and trained in its use, before being sent to France in the summer of 1944. Each battalion boasted 12 vehicles divided into three batteries, but only 60 saw frontline service in France and 14 were held in reserve to replace losses.

THE M10 TANK DESTROYER

This turreted tank destroyer was the first tracked vehicle of its type to be put into service by the Americans. First produced in 1942, it made good use of a number of the Sherman's mechanical and structural components, particularly the hull and the tracks and rollers, so as to ease production.

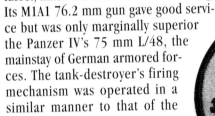

A picture of the M1A1 76.2 mm gun's breechblock. The optical sight is just off camera to the left. Optical sights used by the Allies were somewhat inferior to those used by the Germans.
(National Archives)

....

Right: A sleeve badge as worn from September 1942 onwards by the personnel of tank-destroyer units. (Militaria Magazine)

....

Below: Variants of the M10 were distinguished mainly by different power units and turret shapes.
(National Archives)

Only the turret and the chassis superstructure were new concepts. The hull and turret were designed so that additional armor could be bolted on should the vehicle be called upon to perform the role of combat tank. Additional armor was rarely used, however, as the additional weight affected the tank's performance. The turret was sleek with sloped armor pitched to deflect incoming rounds. Nevertheless the relative thinness of the armor and the open-top turret, made the crew vulnerable during combat.

Its M1A1 76.2 mm gun gave good service but was only marginally superior the Panzer IV's 75 mm L/48, the mainstay of German armored forces. The tank-destroyer's firing mechanism was operated in a similar manner to that of the

The M10 was bestowed a number of nicknames, including the Achilles, the Wolverine or the Slugger. Used in action almost as much as the assault tanks, they sustained heavy casualties.
(Illustration by Jean Restayn)

Sherman, either mechanically or electrically. The chief problem with the M10 was the thickness of the armor; in order to be successful, the vehicle had to get a shot in first before rapidly disengaging. Its rate of fire was 10 rounds a minute. The M10 was produced in great numbers and was mainly supplied to specialist tank-destroyer battalions, each being issued 14 vehicles. These were attached to heavy and light armored divisions and used to support armor or infantry.

Opposite: The M10 could fire a shell capable of penetrating armor 119 mm thick from a range of 900 m. (National Archives)

Right: Polaroid All-Purpose goggles. These were favored by tank crews. (P. Charbonnier Collection)

THE M18 TANK DESTROYER 'HELLCAT'

It was a long time coming but when this tank destroyer finally put in an appearance in early 1944, it quickly demonstrated significant merit and proved itself to be one of the best-armored vehicles fielded by the Allies in World War II.

Hellcats were equipped with three different types of gun. There was the M1A1 without muzzle break or the M1A1C and M1A2 with muzzle breaks. The Hellcat's anti-tank projectile could penetrate 175 mm thick armor from 900m. (National Archives)

Above, right: a US fatigue cap with the distinctive yellow and green piping used to signify armored personnel (not those in the cavalry or mechanized artillery). (J. P. André Collection)

One of its more distinguishing features was its ability to alter the tension of its tracks if faced with difficult terrain. This could be done by means of adjusting the first of the five rollers. The vehicle had relatively thin armor, just 25 mm thick, sloped towards the front, and again, had an open turret. The M18 had a 76.2 mm gun which could pierce armor to a thickness of 175 mm from a distance of 900 m, something that put it into a league of its own. Steering was operated through a central mechanism much like that used in German tanks. The M18 boasted automatic transmission and thanks to its powerful engine, a very favorable ratio of power to weight, making it one of the fastest tracked vehicles to be produced in the war. However, traveling at speed proved so uncomfortable for the unfortunate crew that this advantage was rarely utilized. The Hellcat arrived in Normandy in July 1944 and, thanks to its speed, it went into action in record time. Its pace was often so quick as to completely phase enemy artillery and it earned a fearsome reputation among the Germans.

The Hellcat was one of the most distinctive armored vehicles of the war, but despite its apparent qualities, it was only produced

A Hellcat belonging to the 630th Tank Destroyer Battalion. This unit knocked out 53 enemy tanks (including Panthers and Tigers) and 15 self-propelled guns in July 1944. All that for the loss of seventeen M18s. (Illustration by Jean Restayn)

TECHNICAL DATA

Crew: 5
Combat weight: 17.7 tons
Engine: Continental R975 C4, 9-cylinder gasoline engine, 460 hp
Max. speed on road: 80 km/h
Range on road: 161 km
Fuel capacity: 750 liters
Length with gun: 6.65 m
Length without gun: 5.28 m
Width: 2.87 m
Height: 2.57 m
Armament: 1 x 76 mm M1A1, M1A1c or M1A2, 1 x 12.7 mm M2HB anti-aircraft machinegun
Ammunition: 45 shells, 800 mg rounds
Armor thickness (max.): 25 mm
Radio: SCR 610

in relatively insignificant numbers (by American standards) - a mere total of 2,500. Each tank-destroyer battalion issued with the M18 boasted 14 Hellcats.

O pposite: A metal can used to pour engine oil. (J. P. André Collection)

B elow: The Hellcat carried 75 anti-tank projectiles and 25 HE projectiles. (National Archives)

P receding page: The base of the Hellcat's turret was fitted with a shot-deflector to minimize the vehicle's shot-trap. (National Archives)

The M5A1 Light Tank

This diminutive tank was considered to be out-of-date by 1943 but it continued to be America's most prolific reconnaissance vehicle beyond that date. Consequently, it was the most common light tank employed in reconnaissance units attached to armored regiments.

The M5A1 was produced in massive quantities and was much appreciated by the troops. Its crew were attached to the vehicle on account of its reliability, the ease with which it could be maintained, its mobility (it had an excellent weight to power ratio), its acceleration and its speed (35 miles an hour due to its two Cadillac motors), It was indeed the fastest tank in service until the arrival of the M18 and M24.

The tank made use of a hydramatic gearbox linked up to the motors by a propeller shaft. The interior space had been carefully planned. The tank's body was lined with rubber by way of insulation and to protect the crew. The crew sat on ergonomic seats within the cabin. Gaps between the armor plating of the hull were plugged and lined, making them watertight. Communication was by means of intercom.

The tank was equipped with the M6 37 mm gun fitted with a gyro-stabilizer; the gun was remarkably accurate, even when the tank was in motion. The tracks were extremely secure and it was rare for the tank to lose one. Like the Sherman, the M5A1 had a choice of track according to the type of terrain it encountered. The basic hull was welded together and the glacis plate and rear of the tank were subsequently bolted on. On the other hand, the tank's qualities were almost outweighed by its faults. Its armament was simply outclassed and its silhouette was too high.

A protective cover for the M5's 37 mm gun.
(J. P. André Collection)

Following pages: A 7.62 mm,. 30 M1919 A4 machine gun as used on American tanks.
(Private Collection)

B elow: An M5 at Château-Gontier.
The tactic of reconnaissance by fire, in which tanks would open up on potential targets to flush out the enemy, used up ammunition. As space inside was limited it wasn't unknown for the crew to ride on the outside of the tank so that the interior could store extra ammo.
(National Archives)

TECHNICAL DATA

Crew: 4
Combat weight: 15.5 tons
Engine: Continental 2 x Cadillac series 42, 8 cylinder gasoline engine, 148 hp
Max. speed on road: 58 km/h
Range on road: 161 km
Fuel capacity: 405 liters
Length without gun: 4.84 m
Width: 2.29 m
Height: 2.57 m
Armament: 1 x 37 mm M6 gun, 3 x 7.62 mm M1919 A4 machineguns
Ammunition: 147 shells, 6.750 MG rounds
Armor thickness (max.): 44 mm
Radio: SCR 508/528/538

*D*espite being obsolete by 1944 the M5 would continue to serve until the end of the war in Europe even though the M24 Chaffee, the M5's replacement, had come into service in December 1944. *(Illustration by Jean Restayn)*

In addition, its tracks were too narrow to enable it to cross soft ground. Along with the Sherman, it was equipped with hedge-cutters to allow it to operate in the bocage during Operation Cobra. Each armored regiment in a heavy armored division operated 57 M5A1s whilst those in light armored divisions had 17.

*O*pposite: The use of the M5 in Normandy owed something, perhaps, to the large number of such tanks available. *(National Archives)*

THE M8 ARMORED CAR

Officially designated the Armored Utility Car, this armored vehicle was used throughout the Army. Originally it was conceived as a rapid anti-tank vehicle but by 1944, such a role was no longer viable as the weakness of its armor and armament meant that it could no longer perform in an armored combat role.

The M8's 37 mm gun was traversed manually, as was the turret. Fortunately the turret was light and easy to rotate. (National Archives)

This microphone was used by tank crews to communicate with one another. The microphone was placed inside the mouth to eliminate surrounding noise. (J. P. André collection)

The silhouette of the M8 was low and sleek, allowing it to go to ground relatively easily, and the vehicle's overall appearance was graceful. The vehicle was based on a welded hull, with armor plate 19 mm thick, and a manual-traverse open-topped turret with a 37 mm anti-tank gun. The open-top allowed the crew greater visibility to pinpoint targets and also allowed greater freedom of movement. In later models of the M8 the turret could in fact be covered with a tarpaulin during inclement weather, which kept the rain out and on occasion, the odd grenade. The commander and the co-driver benefited from wide entry hatches and these also provided exceptionally good visibility. Again the vehicle had an excellent weight to power ratio and on a good road, the M8 could reach speeds of 88 km/h, a little faster than its German rivals. Its six wheels gave the vehicle stability and it was rare that an M8 overturned. However crossing rugged terrain created unique problems for the vehicle due to the absence of independent suspension and

TECHNICAL DATA

Crew: 4
Combat weight: 7.73 tons
Engine: Hercules JXD,
6-cylinder gasoline engine,
110 hp
Max. speed on road: 88 km/h
Length: 5.08 m
Width: 2.56 m
Height: 2.26 m
Armament: 1 x 37 mm M6 anti-tank gun
Ammunition: 80 shells,
1,575 mg rounds
Armor thickness (max.):
20 mm
Radio: SCR 510/528

*R*ight: Disk worn on the collars
of US armored personnel.
(Militaria Magazine)

....

*O*pposite: The M8's crew
consisted of a driver,
seated to the left and operating
a standard steering wheel,
a co-driver and radio-operator
to his right
and, in the turret, a gunner
and a gun-loader.
(National Archives)

*A*n M8 Armored Car belonging to the 82nd Reconnaissance Battalion
of the 2nd Armored Division. The M8 carried a good quantity of ammunition.
There were 80 shells and 1,575 rounds for the machine guns. This meant that
a certain amount of equipment had to be carried on the outside of the vehicle.
(Illustration by Jean Restayn)

the fragile nature of that suspension. The fuel tank had a capacity of
212 liters, which gave the vehicle an excellent range.

The M8 could be put together relatively cheaply which made it easy
to mass-produce. It was light, nimble and quiet and was therefore much
utilized by cavalry squadrons (there were 68 in each squadron). One of
its major faults was that it had a tendency to burst into flames upon impact.
Strangely, the vehicle was not provided
with a reverse gear, which meant that things
could get difficult if it chanced across
a more powerful enemy. During the fighting in Normandy the M8 was largely
employed for escort duties, reconnaissance and patrols. It was also used
to a limited degree by the British.

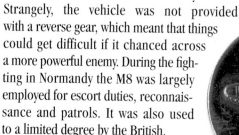

THE M20 ARMORED CAR

The Armored Utility Car M20 was a variant M8 and was produced at the request of Tank Destroyer Command, which wanted an armored vehicle, which could serve as a command car or a troop, ammunition or equipment carrier.

S leeve badge worn by the 4th Cavalry Group. This unit participated in the Normandy campaign.
(Militaria Magazine)

A Colt 45 automatic pistol. This was the best firearm of its type in service and was popular among tank crews.

Such a role, quite different from its predecessor the M8, necessitated the removal of the turret and the adaptation of the armament. This was stripped down to a single heavy machine gun (.50, 12.7 mm) mounted on a metal cradle above the open-topped crew compartment. The M20's gasoline-driven Hercules JXD engine had a low compression ratio of 6.5: 1 and could run on low-octane fuel. An improved version, easier to produce and more powerful, began production in July 1943.

The M20 was light, thanks in part to the absence of a turret, and it was the only vehicle of its type, with the exception of the M8, to be able to cross a Class 9 pontoon bridge. But the insufficient armor

(Militaria Magazine)

TECHNICAL DATA

Crew: 4

Combat weight: 7.73 tons

Engine: Hercules JXD, 6-cylinder gasoline engine, 110 hp

Max. speed on road: 88 km/h

Length: 5.08 m

Width: 2.56 m

Height: 2.26 m

Armament: 1 x 12.7 mm M2HB machinegun

Armor thickness (max.): 20 mm

Radio: SCR 510/528

was a major fault, just as it was with the M8, and the vehicle fell victim time and time again to mines. In order to offset this deficiency, the crew loaded sandbags onto the bottom of the vehicle to absorb the blast.

The vehicle's saving grace was its speed, which meant it could accelerate away from peril. As well as being deployed by tank-destroyer units it was also issued to cavalry and armored divisions. The French 2e Division Blindée made use of the vehicle. Some 3,971 were produced before June 1945.

Preceding page: This rear shot of an M20, and the frontal shot opposite, reveals all angles of the vehicle's unique shape. (DR)

Right: A T45 microphone could be secured below the mouth leaving the hands free to operate the radio. (J. P. André Collection)

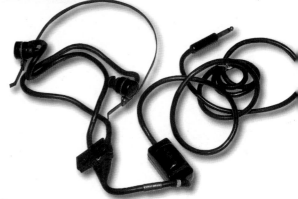

Below: A blackout light used on the M3-M5 and other American vehicles. (J.P. André Collection)

THE M3 AND M5 HALF-TRACK

This vehicle was built to master all types of terrain and was the American equivalent of the German Spw Sd. Kfz. 250/251. Its role was to carry infantry acting in support of tanks.

Two main types of half-track emerged. There was the Car, Half-Track (for reconnaissance purposes) and there was the Carrier, Personnel, Half-Track for transporting troops. The vehicle had sufficient armor to deflect automatic fire and protect the crew from the impact of a shell. Two fuel tanks, each with a capacity of 120 liters, were built into the sides of the vehicle.

The half-track was a front-wheel drive vehicle, which was supposed to prevent it from becoming bogged down in soft ground. Each M3 was equipped with a winch, which could tow up to five tons. To the rear were the tracks. There were four rubber-tired bogies powering tracks and the flexible rubber-padded track plates were a foot wide.

The half-track was a rugged, reliable vehicle, which was cheap and easy to produce and produced it was, in vast numbers. Mechanically it was simple, reliable, and easy to maintain and repair. A popular vehicle, it was generally employed to give infantry mobility and help them keep pace

TECHNICAL DATA

Crew: 3
Capacity: 10 men
Combat weight: 9.1 tons
Engine: White 160 AX or Red Diamond, 6-cylinder gasoline engine, 145 hp
Max. speed on road: 72 km/h
Range on road: 320 km
Fuel capacity: 227 liters
Length: 6.16 m
Width: 1.96 m
Height: 2.30 m
Armament: 1 x 7.62 mm M1919 A4 machinegun and (depending on the version) 1 x 12.7 mm M2HB machinegun
Ammunition: 4,000 - 8,450 MG rounds
Armor thickness (max.): 13 mm
Radio: SCR193/506/508/593/284/ 528/608/610/628

*P*receding page, center: The insignia worn by the French 2ᵉDivision Blindée. (Militaria Magazine)

*P*receding page: This photo was taken at Ecouché on August 19th, 1944, as two half-tracks belonging to the French entered the town. (IWM B9421)

A half-track troop transporter. The machine gun is a .50 M2HB 12.7 mm caliber weapon. There was room for three occupants in the front cab and for five further personnel on either side of the rear compartment. (Illustration by Jean Restayn)

with armored units. In reality it rarely came under fire. Some vehicles were, however, fitted with mantles or protective plates designed to stop grenades from being thrown into the interior. Each mechanized infantry regiment was theoretically issued with 171 half-tracks, 9 went to each cavalry squadron and 27 to each sapper battalion attached to heavy armor divisions. The light armor divisions had the same complement although their infantry battalions had 55 vehicles.

*B*elow: this overcharged half-track at Alençon on August 14th, 1944, of the French 2ᵉ Division Blindée. (National Archives)

THE M16 HALF-TRACK

The M3 troop-carrying half-track gave rise to numerous variants capable of performing a number of roles from transporting munitions to acting as ambulances.

*T*he burnt-out wreck of an M16 on a landing craft. The vehicle probably belonged to the 1st platoon of Battery B, 197th Anti-aircraft Battalion. This unit lost a good deal of its equipment on June 6 when the LCT 200 transporting it was hit by a shell. (National Archives)

....

*O*pposite: An American jerrycan for carrying gasoline. (Private Collection)

....

*B*elow: As well as being employed in defending against aerial attack, the M16 was also used in Normandy against terrestrial targets. (National Archives)

But it was also adapted to carry heavy armament. Some were specifically designed to carry anti-aircraft guns. For example, there was the M15 armed with a 37 mm gun and two 12.7 mm machine guns. Best of all was the M16 with its four 12.7 mm machine guns on a Maxson gun mount.

This vehicle was the main anti-aircraft defense for the Americans in Normandy. The M16 was introduced to protect convoys and strategic points from raids by German fighter-bombers.

As the M16's sides didn't fold down, apart from a slender panel running along the top, the machine guns were mounted on a raised Maxson gun mount, giving the guns an elevation of between 85 and -5 degrees and allowing the guns

*E*ach anti-aircraft battalion comprised eight M16s.
(Illustration by Jean Restayn)

TECHNICAL DATA

Crew: 5
Combat weight: 9.1 tons
Engine: White 160 AX
or Red Diamond,
6-cylinder gasoline engine,
147 hp
Max. speed on road: 68 km/h
Range on road: 320 km
Fuel capacity: 227 liters
Length: 6.52 m
Width: 2.16 m
Height: 2.38 m
Armament: 4 x 12.7 m m
M2HB anti-aircraft
machineguns
Ammunition: 5,000 MG
rounds
Armor thickness (max.):
12.7 mm
Radio: SCR 510/528

to rotate 360 degrees. They really could fire in all directions and, with a rate of fire of 4,500 rounds a minute and a range of 6.8 km, they were deadly.

Generally, two men served the guns, feeding in ammo, will a third aimed and fired.

The vehicle was a real success and 2,877 were produced between May 1943 and March 1944.

*R*ight: A technical manual for half-tracks published in 1944. (J. P. André Collection)

....

*O*pposite: The M15 was the other kind of half-track which could be used in an anti-aircraft role. This one is pictured before the Normandy landings during an exercise in Great Britain.
(National Archives)

PRACTICAL INFORMATION

This information focuses on places which saw armored combat or where substantial numbers of tanks played a part in the battle for Normandy. Military-vehicle enthusiasts should note that we list places where actual vehicles can be seen as well bigger museums and commemorative monuments.

CALVADOS

At Port-en-Bessin there is a **unique museum** of underwater artefacts. It is unique in that it presents items dredged up from the sea-bed: tanks, trucks and other vehicles. It's a novel way of rendering homage to the liberators.

○ *Musée des épaves sous-marines du débarquement*
Route de Bayeux – BP Commes
14520 Port-en-Bessin
Tel: 02 31 21 17 06

Open everyday from June to 30 September. Open weekends in May, 10.00 to 12.00 and 14.00 to 18.00.

Also worth a visit: three plaques and two steles

Some five miles to the south is Bayeux with its **Battle of Normandy Memorial Museum**. It evokes the 77 days of the campaign, has three galleries and covers a large area. Around a hundred uniforms are on display as well as a **Sherman tank**, an **M10 Tank Destroyer**, a **Churchill** and a **Hetzer** (an interesting vehicle which, however, was not deployed in Normandy). There's also a cinema (150 seat-cinema) showing short films on the campaign.

○ *Musée-Mémorial de la Bataille de Normandie*
Boulevard Fabian Ware - BP 21215
14402 Bayeux CEDEX
Tél.: 02 31 92 93 41 - fax: 02 31 21 85 11
www.mairie-bayeux.fr.

Open all year. From 17 September to 30 April, 10.00 to 12.30 and 14.00 to 18.00. From 1 May to 16 September, 09.30 to 18.30. Closed in the second half of January.

Also worth a visit: general de Gaulle's Museum, British Cemetery, monuments, steles and plaques.

From Bayeux head west to Saint-Laurent-sur-Mer. There, not far from Omaha Beach, and close by the American cemetery at Colleville, is the **Omaha Beach Memorial Museum**. Apart from countless artefacts, uniforms and weapons from D-day there are also important records relating to the Resistance and Deportation and details of the economic plight of the region under the Germans. An excellent panorama recreates the landings whilst a **Sherman** and a **155 mm Long Tom** can be seen in the car park as well as a **landing craft**.

○ *Musée d'Omaha Beach à Saint-Laurent-sur-Mer*
« Les moulins » - rue de la mer
14710 Saint-Laurent-sur-Mer
Tél.: 02 31 21 97 44 - fax: 02 31 92 72 80
http://www.museememorial-omaha.com

Open from 15 February to 15 March (10.00 to 12.30 and 14.30 to 18.00), 16 March to 15 May (9.30 to 18.30), 16 May to 15 September (09.30 to 19.00 except July-August: 9.30 to 19.30) and from 15 September to 15 November (9.30 to 18.30).

The American cemetery at Saint Laurent/Colleville might also be of interest with its commemorative plaques and monuments.

From Bayeux you can also head east. Five miles to the north-east is the **Arromanches Museum**, built by the site of the Mulberry harbour. There's a **half-track**, a **Sherman** and **two artillery guns**. The diorama, models, films and exhibits cover the whole of Overlord.

○ *Musée du débarquement d'Arromanches*
Place du 6 juin
14117 Arromanches
Tél.: 02 31 22 34 31 - fax: 02 31 92 68 83
www.normandy1944.com

Open all year round (except January): from 10.00 to 12.30 and 13.30 to 17.00. In summer opening hours are 09.00 to 19.00.

The **360 ° museum at Arromanches** is also of interest.

Five miles to the east of Arromanches in the centre of Ver-sur-Mer, by the D 514, is a **British Sexton**. The museum of the **America-Gold Beach** is also here. There are two buildings and exhibits describe the landings as well as the role of the 50th Division in King sector, Gold Beach.

○ *Musée America-Gold Beach*
2, place Amiral Byrd
14114 Ver-sur-Mer
Tél. fax: 02 31 22 58 58

Opening hours:
From 10.30 to 13.30 and 14.30 to 17.30 in July and August.
Wednesdays and Thursdays (09.30 to 12.00) from 1 November to 30 April. Closed Tuesdays in May, June, September and October.

Also worth a visit: two monuments, two plaques and a board.

Again to the east is Courseulles-sur-Mer with its **monument to the Royal Winnipeg Rifles** and, close to the sea front, a **Sherman tank** restored in 1970. There are also a number of plaques and monuments in the town. In the adjoining town of Graye-sur-Mer there is a **British Churchill mortar** tank near the Liberation monument.

Six miles from Courseulles, at Lion-sur-Mer, there is a **Churchill AVRE** at the western exit of the town on the D 514. In the neighboring town of Hermanville-sur-Mer, and again by the D 514, there is a **British Centaur** and the **British cemetery** with its 1,005 graves and four monuments.

Not far from the beach at Ouistreham, is the **Atlantic Wall Museum**. This is located in a vast bunker, the former HQ commanding all the batteries along the Orne estuary. It gives the visitor a real insight into the way such defences functioned. The rooms are on five levels and have been fitted out just as they were. There are boiler rooms, sleeping quarters, a pharmacy, a hospital, magazines, communication rooms and an observation post fitted with a powerful range-finder.

○ *Musée du bunker du Mur de l'Atlantique*
Boulevard du 6 juin
14150 Ouistreham-Riva-Bella
Tél.: 02 31 97 28 69 - fax: 02 31 96 66 05
e. mail: bunkermusée@aol.com

Opening hours:
10.00 to 18.00 from 3 February to 15 November
09.00 to 19.00 from 1 April to 30 September
Closed 16 November to 2 February